WITHDRAWN

Cori Plays Football

Written by Christine Florie

Illustrated by Christine Tripp

Children's Press®
A Division of Scholastic Inc.
New York • Toronto • London • Auckland • Sydney
Mexico City • New Delhi • Hong Kong
Danbury, Connecticut

For Corinne and all girls who want to play football.
— C.F.

For my grandsons Brandon, Kobe, and Reese.
— C.T.

Consultant

Eileen Robinson
Reading Specialist

Library of Congress Cataloging-in-Publication Data
Florie, Christine, 1964-
  Cori plays football / written by Christine Florie ; illustrated by Christine Tripp.
    p. cm. — (A Rookie reader)
  Summary: Cori wants to join the football team, and she scores a touchdown at tryouts.
  ISBN 0-516-24864-2 (lib. bdg.)   0-516-25023-X (pbk.)
  [1. Football—Fiction.] 2. Sex role-Fiction.]   I. Tripp, Christine, ill. II. Title. III. Series.
PZ7.FCor 2005
[E]—dc22

2004030129

CHILDREN'S PRESS and A ROOKIE READER®, and associated logos are trademarks and or registered trademarks of Scholastic Library Publishing. SCHOLASTIC and associated logos are trademarks and or registered trademarks of Scholastic Inc.

1 2 3 4 5 6 7 8 9 10 R 14 13 12 11 10 09 08 07 06 05

Cori wanted to play football.

"Girls can't play football,"
said her sister Peg.

"Be a cheerleader like me!"

Cori's dad took her to
the field for tryouts.

8

"Cori, you need a helmet, shoulder pads, and knee pads," said Coach Winters.

"Here is a mouth guard to protect your teeth and braces."

Would she be able to play
with all that padding?

Would the boys think she ran like a ballerina?

This shouldn't be so hard to do. Dad and I watch football every season, Cori thought.

We play football all the time, too.

"Just do your best,"
said Cori's dad.

21

Everyone trying out for the team
had to pass a punting test,

a running test,

and a catching test.

Now it was Cori's turn.

Cori punted the ball through
the goalpost.

She ran the fastest up the field.

Now she needed to catch the ball.
Everybody was watching.

Cori caught the ball.

She scored a touchdown!
Everyone cheered.

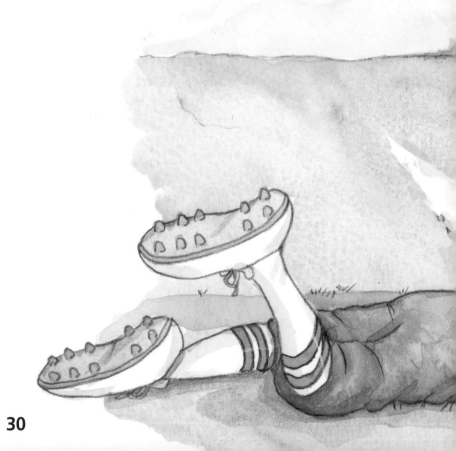

Word List (94 words)

(Words in **bold** are compound words.)

a	dad	it	running	to
able	do	just	said	too
all	every	knee	scored	took
and	**everybody**	like	season	**touchdown**
ball	**everyone**	me	she	trying
ballerina	fastest	mouth	shoulder	**tryouts**
be	field	need	shouldn't	turn
best	**football**	needed	sister	up
boys	for	now	so	wanted
braces	girls	out	team	was
can't	**goalpost**	padding	teeth	watch
catch	guard	pads	test	watching
catching	had	pass	that	we
caught	hard	Peg	the	Winters
cheered	helmet	play	think	with
cheerleader	her	protect	this	would
Coach	here	punted	thought	you
Cori	I	punting	through	your
Cori's	is	ran	time	

About the Author

Christine Florie is a children's book editor and writer who lives in Mahopac, New York, with her husband, two daughters, and black Labrador retriever. When not working, she enjoys going to the beach with her family, reading books, and watching Sunday afternoon football games. She has also written *Braces for Cori* in the *A Rookie Reader* ® series.

About the Illustrator

Illustrator Christine Tripp lives in Ottawa, Canada, with her husband Don; her four grown children Elizabeth, Erin, Emily, and Eric; grandsons Brandon, Kobe, and Reese; three cats; and one very large, scruffy dog named Jake.